Alicia Alonso

Prima Ballerina

By Carmen T. Bernier-Grand

Illustrated by Raúl Colón

Marshall Cavendish Children

To Margery Cuyler, choreographer of this ballet of words—C.B-G.

For all the visionaries at the ballet school in Santa Ana, California, the Wooden Floor, who believe all children, especially youth in financial need, deserve a chance to learn something new and unique—R.C.

Acknowledgments

My thanks to those who helped me write and research this book,
among them: Dr. Miguel Cabrera, Lucía González, Barbara Hansen, Yanelys Márquez,
Ariel & Hilda Lavandera, José Ramón & Cristy Marcos, Conchita Díaz Páez,
Clara & Larry Yust, Pedro Simón & his staff at Museo de la Danza,
Fernando Alonso, Alicia Alonso, Kelly Davio, Kobbie Alamo, and Margarita Engle

Text copyright © 2011 by Carmen T. Bernier-Grand
Illustrations copyright © 2011 by Raúl Colón
All rights reserved
Marshall Cavendish, 99 White Plains Road, Tarrytown, NY 10591
www.marshallcavendish.us/kids

Library of Congress Cataloging-in-Publication Data

Bernier-Grand, Carmen T.
Alicia Alonso : prima ballerina / by Carmen T. Bernier-Grand ; illustrated
by Raúl Colón. —1st ed.
p. cm.
Includes bibliographical references.
ISBN 978-0-7614-5562-2 (hardcover)   ISBN 978-0-7614-5994-1 (e-book)
1. Alonso, Alicia, 1921- 2. Ballerinas. I. Colón, Raúl. II. Title.
GV1785.B348B47 2011
792.8'028092—dc22
[B]
2010018269

The illustrations are rendered in watercolor, colored pencils, and lithograph pencils on watercolor paper.
Book design by Anahid Hamparian
Editor: Margery Cuyler

Printed in China (E)
First edition
1 3 5 6 4 2

Contents

Unga

Born: Marianao, Cuba, December 21, 1921

• • •

Family and friends call her Unga.
She's a child of Hungarian gypsy grace.
Her real name is
Alicia Ernestina de la Caridad del Cobre Martínez y del Hoyo.

Five-year-old Alicia
wraps herself in tulles.
The hem of her blue-sky tunic
is a fluffy cloud.
Like light,
she's barely aware
of the floor beneath her dancing feet.

Mamá: Ernestina del Hoyo

A magician with the needle,
Mamá sews dresses for her daughters,
knits fine lacework on their hems.
Mamá recites poems to the rhythm
of knitting needles,
daughter Cuca hums like a *zunzuncillo*,
daughter Alicia whistles, "*Chui, chui.*"
"Having Mamá near me," Alicia says,
"is like being surrounded by jingle bells."

Papá: Doctor Antonio Martínez

A veterinarian.
A genius with horses.
"Papá is a good man," Alicia says.
"He helps poor *guajiros.*"
"*¿Cafecito, Doctor?*" they ask.
He doesn't charge the *guajiros.*
He drinks their *cafecito* instead.
Doctor Martínez tells his two sons,
"Wear jackets to the dinner table."
To his daughters he says, "Wear dresses.
Make sure your hair is always combed."
His sons will go to college and have jobs.
His daughters will marry and have children.
After dinner, his wife recites poetry,
his sons, Antonio and Elizardo, sing,
his older daughter, Cuca, hums,
his younger daughter, Unga, whistles,
and he falls asleep in his rocking chair.

Flamenco

Jerez de la Frontera and Sevilla, Spain, 1928

• • •

Papá buys horses for the Cuban army.
Alicia and Cuca take flamenco classes.
Alicia wants to wear her teacher's ruffled
skirts of splashing colors, her swaying mantilla.
"*¡Olé! —*the teacher says —. *¡Baile!*"
Alicia and Cuca imitate
the *tatatá* of their teacher's tapping feet,
the *teketé* of her castanets.
At night, Alicia loops the chords of her brown
castanets over her thumbs, wears them to bed.
¡Olé!

Ballet Lessons

Havana, Cuba, 1931

• • •

Alicia takes ballet lessons from Nikolai Yavorsky.
He walks down the line of girls at the dance barre.
With a long stick, he taps Alicia's knees.
"Straight knees, my pupil."
He taps her stomach. "In."
Nikolai Yavorsky sits on a folding chair.
"Backs flat. Stomachs in. Stretch up.
Up! Heads down and straight.
Shoulders down."
Alicia's ribbons slip from her hair.
"No, head up, not back. Down! Neck up."
Unga's muscles are elastic bands stretched tight.
Crystal beads of sweat roll down her chest.
Yavorsky doesn't select her to dance
in *Sleeping Beauty.*

Cenicienta

Girl after girl tries on the pair of pink satin toe shoes.
They fit nobody—but Alicia!
She stands *en pointe.*
"I'm standing on my toes,
on my toes!"

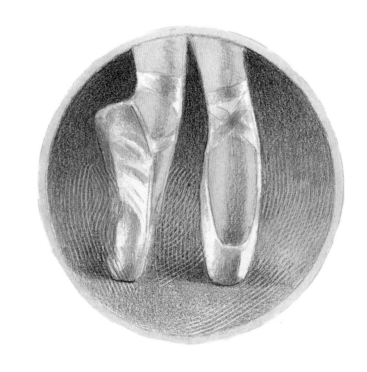

Grand Waltz

Alone.
Alicia dances,
hands overhead,
fingertips forming
a *mariposa* blossom.
Slowly her fingers unfurl.
She whirls.
Her eyes meet Yavorsky's.
"Good." He changes his mind.
"I want you to waltz in *Sleeping Beauty.*"

December 29, 1931

• • •

A lady of the court in *Sleeping Beauty.*
Alicia tries to flip the fan open.
¡Zas! The fan stays shut.
¡Zas, zas, zas!—"Please!"
With coquettish eyes, she looks at the audience,
taps her cheek with the tip of the closed fan,
and waltzes.
The audience laughs and applauds.

First Solo

Her feet hurt.
Her legs hurt.
Her arms hurt.
But ballet dancing
tastes better
than chocolate ice cream.

December 1932

• • •

Alicia's first solo—
a bluebird spinning
and fluttering in a light,
airy flight.
A dance for Princess Aurora
who has been asleep for a hundred years,
and for the prince,
who has woken her up with a kiss.

Coppélia

Yavorsky chooses
Alicia for the role of Swanilda,
Alberto Alonso for the role of Franz.
Lights go on.
At thirteen, Alicia becomes Swanilda,
daughter of the village baker,
in love with Franz
who is in love with Coppélia.
Franz doesn't know Coppélia is a doll.
Swanilda dresses as Coppélia,
dances like a doll.

The hall shakes with applause.
The curtain drops.
Alicia is still Swanilda, still married to Franz.
The audience calls to applaud them.
Alberto holds her hand, takes her to front stage.
Long hands over her heart, she bows,
now Alicia again.

Fernando Alonso

Nineteen.
Sits in the audience.
Watches Alicia and Alberto dance in *Coppélia*.
"My God! Alicia is crazy about dancing.
Someday she will be a great ballerina."
His brother, Alberto, looks elegant. Manly.
"Someday," Fernando tells himself,
"I'd like to dance like that."
He goes to Yavorsky and takes
his first ballet lesson.

Flaming Souls

In the morning,
as their steps join,
Alicia wants Fernando
to be her *danseur*,
her noble danseur.
By noon, their souls flame red.
She'll be the sun,
he'll be the moon in *"Clair de Lune."*
At evening's end, they talk.
Yavorsky has taught all the steps he can.
There is no other school in Cuba.
No ballet company.
With each step they take away from the studio,
Fernando Alonso steps closer to New York.
Sprinkled by the breaking sea on the Malecón,
he asks her: "For the love of God, will you join me?"

Leaving Behind a Blue Childhood

"To be a professional ballet dancer is fit only
for prostitutes," Papá says. "Ballet
is for girls to learn poise, grace, and good posture."
"In New York I will *just* study ballet," Alicia says.
"You are not married," Mamá says. "People will talk."
"As soon as I arrive in New York, I will marry
Fernando," Alicia promises.
"Fifteen is too young to get married. And married to a *male*
ballet dancer!" Papá protests.
"From a good family," Mamá reminds him.
With a *Pa'lante* and blessings from Mamá,
Alicia leaves behind her childhood.
Good-bye, oh my Cuba, good-bye. *¡Ay!*

New York City

New York.

>Alicia arrives with a round tummy, feet pointing out,
>until her baby is born.

New York.

>Alicia holds tight to Fernando.
>Fernando speaks fluent English.

New York.

>Alicia Martínez marries Fernando
>and becomes Alicia Alonso.

New York.

>Fernando and Alicia rent an apartment,
>and its living room becomes a ballet studio.

New York.

>Fernando is accepted into the corps of ballet
>doing the peasant dance in *Giselle.*

New York.

>Laurita makes Alicia a mother
>and Fernando says, "What a beautiful baby girl!"

Debut on an American Stage

Alicia *must* take ballet lessons.
Twenty-five cents a class!
She leaves her newborn with a neighbor.
Most dancing jobs are for Broadway musicals, not ballet.

Alicia auditions to tap-dance in *Great Lady.*
Taps flamenco!
The director roars with laughter.
"I want that girl in all the shows I do."

Ballet Caravan

Good news:
Alicia and Fernando will dance
with Ballet Caravan.
Bad news:
One-year-old Laurita cannot go on tour.
Thirty-five shows, ten long weeks
across country on a bus.
Alicia and Fernando send Laurita
to her grandparents in Cuba.

Alicia and Fernando put on
the red, white, and blue ballet shoes
to dance the rhythms of the United States.
One and two and three . . .
Alicia stands out.
Dances to her own timing.
Plays a grace in *Three Graces with Satyr,*
a passerby in *City Portrait,*
a saloon girl in *Billy the Kid.*
"Did you see that arabesque?" one dancer asks.
"Sensational!" Alicia hears.
What is so sensational when she has had to send Laurita away?

Laurita's Second Birthday

Havana, Cuba, March 18, 1940

• • •

Alicia and Fernando rush
to the island where the sun reigns
and sugarcane blooms like sea spume.
Kisses and embraces.
Laurita has blossomed,
a gleeful *mariposa.*
Alicia and Fernando dance for her
in the salty fragrance of the Caribbean Sea.
They leave Laurita in Cuba,
but they tell her they will return soon.

Pesky Speck

Ballet Theater accepts Alicia!
Alicia is a cygnet in *Swan Lake*.
She links hands with other swans.
Legs go *tan-tan-tan tara tara tan-tan*.
A dark speck floats in Alicia's right eye.
Please, go away.
Tan! Tan! Taán! Tan Tan!
Alicia keeps dancing.
After her performance in *Swan Lake*,
a solo in *Peter and the Wolf*.
Birdlike elbows flow back,
arms flutter, wings in flight.

Alicia bumps into things at home,
but she keeps dancing.
Turning and rapid stepping
—*parará-parará*—
she dances in *Le Grand Pas de Quatre*.
Seventeen curtain calls.
Seventeen!

Swarming Darkness

Dancing in a full theater.

More pesky specks in her eyes.

A sparkle flashes on the edge of her right eye.

She stumbles.

The audience gasps.

A gray curtain moves across her eyes.

Her feet slip from under her.

She collapses.

The theater curtain drops.

"You Must Not Cry"

Surgery.
Alicia's right retina is reattached.
A month later, the bandages come off.
> Her right eye has no side vision.
> How can she dance?

> The car she is in pirouettes on the road.
> Dark speck back in Alicia's right eye.
> She stumbles: Another speck in her left eye.
> Fernando is a shadow.

Fernando takes Alicia to Cuba.
A doctor reattaches the two retinas.
"You must not cry," he says.
"You must not laugh. You must not move."
> "How can I stop living?
> Dancing is my life!"

Dancing Fingers

Blindfolded Alicia listens to the music of *Giselle.*
Her fingers are her feet, the bedsheet the stage.
"I see the theater curtain open. I absolutely see it."
> *Giselle is in love with another peasant, Loys.*
Alicia's fingers jump high—Giselle's feet.
> *Giselle learns that Loys is Prince Albrecht in disguise.*
> *As a peasant she cannot marry him. She becomes insane.*
Alicia's fingers move stiffly, horribly distorted.
> *The earth shakes the day Giselle dies.*
> *That evening she becomes a Willi,*
> *a female spirit whose love is unfulfilled.*
Alicia's fingers jump high, but land as silently as spirit feet.
> *In the cold dawn the Willis rise from their graves*
> *to force Albrecht to dance until he dies of exhaustion.*
Alicia's fingers float softly.
> *She doesn't let the Willis touch him.*
> *Giselle's devotion saves Albrecht from death.*
The golden damask curtain closes.
The audience erupts in applause.
Alicia's fingers take a bow.

Raging Storm

Alicia dashes after her Great Dane Liota's puppies.
Palm trees reach to the heavens,
praying for Alicia's safety.
The door quivers and quakes.
Alicia bends down to pick up the dogs.
Clack!
The door comes straight at them.
Thwack!
It hits her back—crashes.
Tears of blood. "*¡Ay, Dios mío*, my eyes!"

"You just have cuts and bruises," the doctor tells her.
"Can I dance?" Alicia asks.
"It's up to you," the doctor says.
Alicia calls Ballet Theater in New York.
"I am ready to return."

To See and Dance

New York, 1942

• • •

Each morning, Alicia practices with Fernando.
To prepare for a spin, he tells her
to straighten her back for better balance.
To avoid dizziness, he tells her to focus on a fixed spot.
She has no side vision. She cannot spot to spin!
Fernando stands with a flashlight.
Alicia focuses on the light. She spins. Flawless!
Before a lift,
he stretches out his arms to catch her,
but she misses.
On the next try, he makes clicking sounds.
She follows the sounds, lands in his arms.
"God does not intend that
I take for granted these fine gifts:
to see, to dance."

No Way

Alicia watches Markova
rehearse *Giselle.*
Anton Dolin
plays Prince Albrecht.
In October, Markova
becomes very ill.
Who can replace Markova?
Alicia waits to be asked.
Dolin asks two other ballerinas.
Only five days
to learn all the steps.
They say, "No way!"
Dolin turns to Alicia.
"Yes," she says, "I'll dance."

Dancing Feet

Metropolitan Opera House, New York City, November 2, 1943

• • •

Backstage.
Five full days of rehearsals.
Alicia rotates her ankles,
bandages her badly blistered feet

Onstage.
She dances a flirting, sometimes shy Giselle.
She's not dancing it her own way.
Moving one burning foot in front of the other,
imitates Markova's en pointes and turns.
Finale.
The audience is on its feet.
Alicia's feet are shards of broken glass.

Backstage.
She unlaces her ballet shoes, but cannot take them off.
Dry blood has glued her toe shoes to her feet.
A ballet collector offers to help,
removes her ballet shoes carefully.
He runs away with them.
"For history! For history!"

Doctor Martínez

Papá sees photos of a ballerina in *Life* magazine.
Alicia! His daughter—a professional ballet dancer?
A photo caption reads: "One of the prettiest figures in ballet."
Papá buys every issue of *Life* magazine in Havana.
Proudly, he gives them to family and friends.

Undertow

Markova returns, and Alicia loses the role of Giselle.
I'll never be that good, Alicia tells herself.
Alicia works alone before class.
Alicia works with fellow dancers in class.
Alicia works alone after class.
Alicia works on weekdays.
Alicia works on weekends.

New York, 1945

• • •

Alicia is Ate in *Undertow*.
She makes men's skin crawl.
"Go see Alicia Alonso's Ate," many newspapers say.
After *Undertow, Giselle!*
Each step is Alicia's, not Markova's.
"Alicia Alonso," critics agree,
"America's finest Giselle!"

Ballet Alicia Alonso

Cuba, 1948

• • •

Alicia, Fernando, and Alberto
form Ballet Alicia Alonso.
¡Bravo! the audience cheers in Cuba.
¡Bravísimo! the audience cheers in Latin America.
But there is no money
for Alicia's costume in *The Dying Swan.*
"Don't worry," Mamá says. "I'll think of something."
When Alicia returns from rehearsal,
she finds a white tutu spread out on a chair.
"How did you do that?" Alicia asks Mamá.
"The hotel's curtains were too long."
But Mamá cannot do anything
about the scenery sets
—a fire hazard—
and the unpaid ballet dancers.
Alicia appeals to her people:
"Doesn't our government
wish to gain prestige in the world?"
The Cuban government absorbs the ballet's debts
and grants it a small subsidy.

Ballet de Cuba

Cuba, 1950

• • •

Academia Alicia Alonso, a school to teach Cubans ballet.
Fernando is general director; Alberto is artistic director;
Cuca is assistant director; Alicia is principal dancer.
Twelve-year-old Laurita is a student.

Cuba, 1955

• • •

With mostly Cuban dancers,
Ballet Alicia Alonso is renamed Ballet de Cuba.
Dictator Fulgencio Batista wants to control the ballet.
Twenty thousand Cubans protest.
Batista withdraws his support.
No money. No Ballet de Cuba.
Alicia vows not to set her pointes
on the Cuban stage while Batista is in power.
Alicia leaves.
"I cannot live if I do not dance."
Fernando and Laurita stay in Cuba.

The Cuban Revolution

Cuba, January 1, 1959

• • •

Batista

leaves Cuba, his people licking his heels.

Batista,

who calls himself The Man, as if he were the only man in the world.

Batista,

who once jailed Alicia's father for refusing to buy horses for his cruel regime.

Batista,

who took the money away from Ballet de Cuba.

Batista,

who tortured and killed many Cubans.

Batista,

who forced revolutionary Fidel Castro to live in Sierra Maestra.

Batista,

who was supported by the government of the United States.

Batista,

who asked to be exiled to Florida and *¡Jah!* the United States said no—go to Spain.

Batista,

who, for better or worse, would be succeeded by bearded revolutionary Fidel Castro.

Fidel Castro

Fernando, upstairs in his bedroom reading.

Pam-pam-pam-pám.

Who could that be?

Alicia is in Chicago.

Who could be knocking at two in the morning?

Fidel Castro.

They talk for hours.

At last Fidel stands up.

"It's so late. I have an appointment and must go."

He starts downstairs, then stops.

"I forgot what I came for," he says.

"How much money does the ballet need?"

"One hundred thousand dollars," Fernando says.

"I'll give you two hundred thousand dollars,

but it better be a good ballet."

Banned

Alicia must choose:
dance for the United States
or dance for communist Cuba.
"All my hopes and dreams
consist of going out
to the world, taking our flag and art.
My desire is to hear everybody
cheer for Cuba when I dance.
If it cannot be that way,
if that dream cannot be true,
sadness will be the reward for my efforts."
Alicia travels the world.
Her dancing gives life to people.
But in the United States,
she's already dead.

Latin Temptress

Moscow, Russia, April, 1967

• • •

Maya Plisetskaya dances Alberto Alonso's
choreography in *Carmen,*
a black leotard under a sheer gauzy skirt,
an ornate Spanish comb on her head.
Wasn't Alberto Alicia's brother-in-law?
Wasn't Carmen a Latin name?
Didn't Carmen sell *habanos,* Cuban cigars,
as she danced?
Alicia tells Alberto, "You must choreograph *Carmen* for me."

Havana, Cuba, August 1967

• • •

Alicia Alonso dances Alberto Alonso's
choreography in *Carmen,*
red macramé over a beige leotard,
gypsy shoulders and hips, sensuous as a serpent,
eyes like a coquette.
Alberto says, "Maya's *Carmen* is tough, brave, confrontational.
Alicia's *Carmen* is a sensual Latin temptress."

Prima Ballerina Assoluta

Copenhagen, Denmark, 1969

• • •

Rehearsing *Giselle*,
Alicia crashes into the stage cottage.

She counts steps, etches the stage in her mind.
Spotlights of different colors warn her
she is too near the orchestra pit.
She moves, a paintbrush on canvas.
She is not able to see to her right.
She is not able to see to her left.
Her partner, Igor Youskevich,
moves ahead of her so she can see him.
She imagines an axis
and pirouettes across her own inner stage.
Her footwork zigzags through air.
Critics say she's the most moving and sweetest Giselle.
Alicia Alonso *is* prima ballerina *assoluta*.

Beloved Ballerina

Metropolitan Opera House, New York City, 1975

• • •

Alicia Alonso has been invited back to the United States.
Outside Lincoln Center, exiled Cubans picket:
>ALICIA ALONSO
>WHY DO YOU FIND KILLINGS BY CASTRO
>MORE ACCEPTABLE THAN KILLINGS BY BATISTA?
>ALICIA ALONSO
>YOUR SUCCESS COMES FROM SELF-INTEREST.

Alicia's response:
"Artists have roots and my roots are in Cuba."
After the finale of *Swan Lake,*
rhythmical chants shake the hall:
"Alicia! Alicia! Alicia!"
Crying, Alicia Alonso bows.
Her fifteen-year exile has ended in triumph.
In the balcony an American and a Cuban unfurl a banner:
>WELCOME, ALICIA! *¡BIENVENIDA!*

Ballet School

"You must feel the rain," Maître Laura tells her class.
"Aaa-yan, paa-paan."
Even Alicia takes lessons from her daughter.
"You must feel the wind. *Aaa-yan, paa-paan.*"
"Your students are stretching their thighs too much,"
Alicia interrupts.
Maître Laura responds, "You are brilliant, Mamá."
"I'm still learning," says Alicia.
"The day I stop, I cease to grow as an artist."

Farfalia

"I will never announce my last performance,"
    Alicia teases.
"You would have to come to all my appearances
    to see the last one."
Seventy-four-year-old Alicia
    dances *Farfalia.*
The butterfly with visionless vision
    can no longer turn herself, whirl herself.
Male dancers gently whirl her, turn her, lift her.
    How short the lives
of butterflies really are! Farfalia finishes the ballet,
    then flies away.
"That was the last time," Alicia says.
    "But I still dance inside me."

"I Still Have Time"

Although Alicia
is not performing,
she is still
on center stage.
She listens
to the music,
choreographs
in her mind,
explains
to ballet masters.
How would you like
to be remembered?
"I'm telling you,"
Alicia answers.
"There is a future
ahead. Ask me
in two hundred years."

—Alicia Alonso

Prima Ballerina Assoluta

Alicia Ernestina de la Caridad del Cobre Martínez y del Hoya was born near Havana, Cuba, on December 21, 1921, to Antonio Martínez and Ernestina del Hoyo. Alicia's father was a veterinarian who bought, bred, and sold horses for the Cuban Army. Her mother was a homemaker and seamstress.

When Alicia was eight years old, she took her first ballet lesson at the Sociedad Pro-Arte Musical in Havana. Laura Rayneri de Alonso, mother of Alberto and Fernando Alonso, was the manager; Nikolai Yavorsky was the ballet teacher. His students danced in tennis shoes. Some people say that a worthy mother brought the first pair of ballet slippers to Havana, but Alicia once said that an Italian gentleman did. In any case, they fit only Alicia. She hardly took them off, making her father wonder if she would ever walk in regular shoes again.

On December 29, 1931, Alicia had her first debut, a member of the court in *Sleeping Beauty.* In 1932, she danced her first solo as the bluebird in *Sleeping Beauty.*

Alicia was not yet a teenager when Fernando Alonso met her for the first time. On vacation from studying business in the United States, he went to pick up her brother, Antonio, for a party. Alicia answered the door en pointe, wearing her ballet slippers.

On March 20, 1935, Fernando saw Alicia and his brother, Alberto, dance in *Coppélia,* and he decided to learn ballet, too. A year later, he and Alicia danced together in "*Clair de Lune.*" They were very much in love.

In 1937, Alicia and Fernando moved to Spanish Harlem in New York City where they married. Fernando was accepted into the corps of Mordkin Ballet Company, but Alicia could not dance because she was pregnant. On March 18, 1938, she gave birth to Laurita in Manhattan's Women's Hospital.

A few days later, Alicia left Laurita with a neighbor and went to take ballet classes. She took lessons with Alexandra Fedorova, Enrico Zanfretta, and other eminent professors from the School of American Ballet. But the dancing jobs were in musicals, not ballet. Alicia's first professional performance was as a chorus girl in *Great Lady* in 1938 and *Stars in Your Eyes* the following year.

In 1939, Fernando and Alicia sent Laurita home to Cuba, and they joined Ballet Caravan. The company toured the United States, and Alicia became a soloist. Unfortunately, due to financial difficulties, Ballet Caravan was short-lived.

In January 1940, dancer and millionaire Lucia Chase donated money to form Ballet Theater (later American Ballet Theater). Alicia joined the company and was selected for various solos. She received seventeen curtain calls for her role in *Le Grand Pas de Quatre.*

Alicia began to experience difficulties with her vision. She was diagnosed with a detached retina in her right eye. Today laser surgery can reattach retinas, but in the 1940s, surgeons snipped all around the retina to eliminate dead tissue. Alicia had two surgeries at Columbia Presbyterian Hospital in New York City, but she ended up with no side vision in her right eye. Then she had a car accident that caused both retinas to detach.

Her retinas were reattached in Cuba. Some doctors blamed her ailment on fragile capillaries, but a Cuban doctor decided that the cause was tonsillitis. While her eyes were still bandaged, he took her tonsils out, causing a hemorrhage.

Doctors told her that her dance career was over. Nevertheless, as she lay for a year in bed, she practiced ballet in her head, going over the movements of *Giselle* until she knew them by heart. After the bandages were removed, she practiced ballet, hiding in the bathroom. Soon afterward and without her doctor's knowledge, she resumed her dancing with Cuba's Pro-Arte Musical. But in March 1942, she survived a storm largely unharmed, and the doctor gave her permission to dance. She returned to New York and rejoined the Ballet Theater.

On November 2, 1943, Alicia got the break she had been waiting for. Alicia Markova became ill and Alicia Alonso was asked to dance the role of *Giselle.* Alonso's performance was widely acclaimed. She was promoted to principal dancer of Ballet Theater and performed in Tudor's *Undertow* and Balanchine's *Theme and Variations*. She developed a reputation as a dramatic dancer and a skilled interpreter of classic ballet. But after a year, Ballet Theater closed its doors, and Alicia and Fernando returned to Cuba.

On October 28, 1948, Alicia, Fernando, and Alberto founded Ballet Alicia Alonso. Most of its early dancers had been laid off from Ballet Theater. Their luck did not improve with Ballet Alicia Alonso. After a tour in Central and South America, they returned unpaid to the United States. Alicia asked for help. The Cuban government gave her funding and paid the company's debts.

In 1950, the Alonsos founded the Academia de Ballet Alicia Alonso to train Cuban dancers. Five years later Ballet Alicia Alonso, almost completely Cuban, was renamed Ballet de Cuba.

The following year, Dictator Batista announced that he wanted to take control of Ballet de Cuba. After Alicia had rejected his bribes and proposals, the government withdrew funding from the school and company. Alicia vowed not to dance in Cuba while the Batista government was in power. She joined the Ballet Russe of Monte Carlo.

On Christmas 1957, Alicia danced *Giselle* at the Bolshoi of Moscow, becoming the first ballet dancer in the western hemisphere to perform in the Soviet Union. A year later, she danced in *The Nutcracker* with Ballet Russe in Chicago, where she learned that the United States had informed Batista that it could no longer support his regime. On January 1, 1959, before daybreak, Batista left Cuba for Spain. The next day, communist Fidel Castro took control of Cuba.

On April 21, 1960, Alicia danced *Don Quixote* and *Giselle* at the twentieth anniversary of American Ballet Theater. The next January, President Dwight D. Eisenhower severed diplomatic relations with communist Cuba and imposed travel restrictions on all U.S. citizens. Alicia had to choose between living in the United States and living in Cuba. She chose Cuba. Exiled Cubans called her decision despicable. They had fled Cuba because of Castro's repressive dictatorship, and they considered it an insult to their forced exile to have their diva return to Cuba.

Alicia felt Cuba needed her. "I was all over the island, to every one of the tiny mountain villages to find children who wanted to dance."

Jorge Esquivel was one of those children. "We were lucky," he once said. "We had Alicia, the dancer and international figure; we had Fernando, the director and teacher; and we had Alberto, the dancer and choreographer; it was a triangle that helped Ballet Nacional de Cuba move forward." At eighteen, Esquivel became one of Alicia's best ballet partners.

Igor Youskevitch was another one of Alicia's famous partners who, like other noble danseurs, became expert at helping Alicia conceal her vision impediment.

Alicia was nearly blind but nothing of importance was done without her permission. Some people resented her, including Jorge Esquivel, who defected while on a tour to Italy in 1992. "Alicia wanted all the good roles for herself. We were like pawns on a chessboard with her moving us around at her convenience."

In 1974, Alicia and Fernando divorced. "Alicia and I started to have a lot of differences so I left for the Cuban province of Camagüey," he explained.

A year later, Alicia married poet and dance critic Pedro Simón, who had been following her career. Also in 1975, after years of lobbying by friends in the American Ballet Theater, Alicia was invited to dance again in the United States. Many exiled Cubans protested, since they felt betrayed by her choice to live in a communist country that had oppressed them and their families.

But Alicia's performances were praised from New York to Beijing. She did not hang up her ballet shoes until she was seventy-four. "Ah, my pointed slippers," she said. "You can't imagine how much I miss them."

As of spring 2011, she remains in complete control of Ballet Nacional de Cuba, and she still choreographs. Her versions of *Giselle, Le Grand Pas de Quatre,* and *La Fille Mal Gardée* are internationally known. How does she do it? In 1972, Dr. Joaquín Barrager, a doctor in Spain, restored her left eye's vision, but he could not do anything to help her right eye, and now she's loosing sight in her left eye again. How can anybody choreograph with limited vision?

"I imagine the ballets deep in my mind," Alicia says. "I draw them in my head. I feel what the dancer is doing on the stage."

Alicia is ninety years old. She thinks she will live forever, but she won't. What will happen to Ballet Nacional de Cuba when she dies?

Historian Miguel Cabrera answers the question this way: "Do you think Picasso died? Do you think Michelangelo died? Alicia won't ever die because the Cuban ballet won't ever die."

Some of the Hundred and Thirty-two Ballets Danced by Alicia Alonso

A lady of the court in "Great Waltz" (1931) and the bluebird in *Sleeping Beauty* (1932) * Swanilda in *Coppélia* (1935) * The sun in *"Clair de Lune"* (1936) * A grace in *Three Graces with Satyr* (1939) * Mother and Mexican girlfriend in *Billy the Kid* (1939) * *Dioné* (1940) * Corps de ballet and "Pas de Trois" (1940), *Le Grand Pas de Quatre* and "Two Swans" (1941) * "Pas de Deux" (1944) * "Black Swan" (1946) * Maja in *Goyesca* (1940) * Bird in *Peter and the Wolf* (1940) * Grisi in *Le Grand Pas de Quatre* (1941) * *Giselle* (1943) * "Pas de Deux" in *Les Sylphides* (1944) * "Episode from the Past" in *Jardin aux lilas* (1944) * "Pas de Deux" in *Waltz Academy* (1944) * "Pas de Deux" in *Don Quixote* (1944) * "Pas de Deux" in *The Nutcracker* (1945) * Ate in *Undertow* (1945) * *Theme and Variations* (1947) * *La Fille Mal Gardée* (1950) * Odile and Odette in *Swan Lake* (1954) * *Carmen* (1967) * *Un Retablo para Romeo y Julieta* (1969) * *Salomé* (1975) * "Pas de Deux" in *La Peri* (1976) * *Misión Korad* (1980) * *La Diva* (1982) * *Farfalia* (1995)

Some of the Ballets Choreographed by Alicia Alonso

La Condesita (1942) * *La Tinaja* (1942) * *Giselle* (1948) * *Le Grand Pas de Quatre* (1948) * *Les Sylphides* (1948) * *Peter and the Wolf* (1948) * *La Fille Mal Gardée* (1952) * *Swan Lake* (1954) * *Coppélia* (1957) * *Sleeping Beauty* (1974) * *Misión Korad* (1980) * *Dido Abandonada* (1988) * *Don Quijote* (1988) * *Sinfonía de Gottschalk* (1990) * *Retrato de un Vals* (1990) * *Las cuatro estaciones*'s "Invierno" (1993) * *Farfalia* (1995) * *The Nutcraker* (1998) * *En las Sombras de un Vals* (1999) * *Shakespeare and His Masks* (2008).

Some of the Awards and Recognitions Received by Alicia Alonso

Dance Magazine's Annual Award (1934) * *Mademoiselle* magazine's One of Ten Outstanding Women (1946) * Medal of the Order of Carlos Manuel de Céspedes and title of *Dama* (1947) * Grand Prix de la Ville de Paris (1966, 1970, 1999) * Anna Pavlova Award of the University of Dance, Paris (1966) * Gold Medal from El Gran Teatro del Liceo de Barcelona (1971) * Honorary Doctorate of Arts from the University of Havana (1973) * Order of Work of the Democratic Republic of Vietnam (1974) * Ana Betancourt Award, Women's Foundation of Cuba (1974) * Order Felix Valera from the Council of State of the Republic of Cuba (1981) * Proclaimed in Mexico "Prima Ballerina Assoluta of the Americas" (1991) * Great Honor Award, Japan (1991) * Encomienda de la Orden de Isabel la católica by king of Spain Juan Carlos I (1993) * Honorary degree from Universidad Politécnica of Valencia (1998) * Gold Medal from the Círculo of Bellas Artes of Madrid (1998) * Arts & Letters Order, Commander Degree, from the Ministry of Culture and Communication of France (1998) * Order of José Martí by the Council of State of the Republic of Cuba (2000) * UNESCO Goodwill Ambassador (2002) * Gold Medal of Merit in Beaux-Arts from Spanish king Juan Carlos (2008).

1921 On December 21, Alicia Ernestina de la Caridad del Cobre Martínez y del Hoyo is born to Antonio Martínez de la Maza Arreondo and Ernestina del Hoyo y Lugo.

1928 Alicia and her family spend ten months in Jerez de la Frontera and Sevilla, Spain.

1931 Alicia attends Escuela de Ballet de la Sociedad Pro-Arte Musical de la Habana. Laura Rayneri de Alonso is the manager; Nikolai Yavorsky is the teacher. On December 29, Alicia debuts as a member of the court in *Sleeping Beauty.*

1932 Alicia dances her first solo as the bluebird in *Sleeping Beauty.*

1933 On January 14, in a coup, Fulgencio Batista takes over the Cuban government.

1935 On March 20, Alicia dances the role of Swanilda and Alberto Alonso dances the role of Franz in *Coppélia.*

1936 On June 22, Alicia and Fernando Alonso dance together in *"Clair de Lune," "By the Light of the Moon."*

1937 Alicia and Fernando move to Spanish Harlem in New York City and get married. Fernando is accepted into the corps of Mordkin Ballet Company.

1938 On March 18, Alicia gives birth to Laurita in Women's Hospital in New York. Alicia takes ballet lessons from Enrico Zanfretta. Fernando leaves the Mordkin Ballet Company and finds a job in the musical *Three Waltzes.*

1938–1939 Alicia and Fernando dance and sing in the Broadway musicals *Great Lady* and *Stars in Your Eyes.* They take lessons at the School of American Ballet and the academy started by the Russian dancer Alexandra Fedorova.

1939 In the spring, Alicia is accepted into the corps of Lincoln Kirstein's Ballet Caravan. Laurita is sent back to Cuba. Alicia plays the roles of passerby in *City Portrait*, a grace in *Three Graces with Satyr*, and a saloon girl in *Billy the Kid.* Unfortunately, Ballet Caravan is short-lived.

1940 In January, dancer and millionaire Lucia Chase donates money for the Mordkin Ballet to be reorganized and renamed Ballet Theater. On March 4, Alicia dances *Dioné* in Teatro Auditorium, Havana. On March 18, Alicia and Fernando celebrate Laurita's second birthday in Havana. In the spring, Alicia and Fernando return to Ballet Theater in New York City. They study with choreographers George Balanchine and Anthony Tudor, among others. Supported by a coalition of political parties, which includes the old Cuban Communist Party, Fulgencio Batista wins the Cuban presidential elections.

1941 Alicia plays the role of the bird in *Peter and the Wolf.* She receives seventeen curtain calls for her role in *Le Grand Pas de Quatre.* In the spring, Alicia becomes ill during a performance. She suffers from the detachment of the right retina. She undergoes two surgeries at Columbia Presbyterian Hospital in New York City, but she ends up without peripheral vision. She has a car accident in which both retinas detach. They are reattached in Cuba. While blindfolded, she has surgery for tonsillitis. Her doctor advises her to quit dancing.

1942 Without her doctor's permission, Alicia resumes her dancing in Cuba's Pro-Arte. In March, after she survives a storm largely unharmed, the doctor gives her permission to dance. On June 2, she starts dancing again. On October 27, Alicia dances two ballets she has choreographed, *La Tinaja* and *La Condesita*, at the Teatro Auditorium in Havana. Alicia rejoins the Ballet Theater in New York City.

1943 On November 2, Alicia debuts in *Giselle* with Anton Dolin at the Metropolitan Opera House.

1944 On March 20, Alicia is featured in *Life* magazine. Her father buys all the copies he can find in Havana. Ramón Grau is elected president of Cuba. Batista is forced to relinquish control.

1945 On April 10, Alicia plays Ate in *Undertow.* In the fall, Alicia dances *Giselle* at the Metropolitan Opera House in New York.

1947 On November 26, Alicia dances *Theme and Variations* created for her by George Balanchine.

1948 Ballet Theater has financial problems and the 1949 season is canceled. Alicia and Fernando return to Cuba. On October 28, Alicia, Fernando, and Alberto Alonso establish Ballet Alicia Alonso.

1949 In January, Ballet Alicia Alonso tours Central and South America.

1950   The Cuban Ministry of Education provides Ballet Alicia Alonso with a monthly subsidy and a sum of money to pay its debts. The Alonsos establish the Academia de Ballet Alicia Alonso to train new generations of Cubans. As the main dancer of the reopened Ballet Theater, Alicia tours Europe.

1952   In a military coup on March 10, Fulgencio Batista becomes Cuba's dictator again.

1953   In July, Fidel Castro, with more than a hundred followers, storms into Santiago de Cuba. The attack fails and Batista forces the group to live in Sierra Maestra.

1955   Ballet Alicia Alonso, almost completely Cuban, is renamed Ballet de Cuba. Batista wants to control Ballet de Cuba. Alicia rejects his proposals. Alicia joins the Ballet Russe de Monte Carlo and stays with the company until 1960. She dances in the Festival of Jacob's Pillow, one of the most prestigious North American ballet companies.

1956   On September 16, 25 thousand people rally at the University of Havana to protest the government's decision to remove the subsidy for Ballet de Cuba. Although the Academia continues its classes, Alicia decides not to dance in Cuba while the Batista government is in power. Ballet Theater is renamed American Ballet Theater.

1957   On Christmas night, Alicia dances *Giselle* at the Bolshoi of Moscow, becoming the first American from the western hemisphere to dance in the Soviet Union.

1958   In December, Alicia dances "Version in Two Acts" in *The Nutcracker* with Ballet Russe in Chicago. On December 11, the United States informs Batista that it can no longer support his regime. On December 31, before daybreak, Batista leaves Cuba for Spain.

1959   On January 1, Fidel Castro takes control of Cuba. On January 3, he announces he is a communist. In March, Alicia spins thirty-two *fouettés,* dancing the Black Swan in *Swan Lake* in Cuba. In September, Fidel Castro announces a large annual subsidy for Ballet de Cuba. Ballet de Cuba is renamed Ballet Nacional de Cuba. In October, Alicia and Ballet Nacional de Cuba tour Latin America.

1960   On April 21, Alicia dances *Don Quixote* and *Giselle* at the twentieth anniversary of American Ballet Theater. On May 20, Law 812 is passed assuring an annual subsidy for Ballet Nacional de Cuba.

1961   In January, President Dwight D. Eisenhower severs diplomatic relations with Cuba. The U.S. State Department bars Alicia from returning to the United States.

1967   In August, Alicia dances *Carmen* choreographed by Alberto Alonso.

1969   Rehearsing *Giselle* in Denmark, Alicia crashes into the scenery.

1970   Because of her inability to focus, Alicia has to give up her role of the black swan in *Swan Lake.*

1972   In Barcelona, Spain, Dr. Joaquín Barraguer performs surgery and Alicia's left eye regains vision. Her right eye remains permanently without peripheral vision.

1974   Alicia divorces Fernando Alonso.

1975   The U.S. State Department reverses itself and grants Alicia permission to dance again in the United States. In July, Alicia dances in New York City, after an absence from the United States of fifteen years. She marries dance critic Pedro Simón.

1978   The Ballet Nacional de Cuba makes its first appearance in the United States.

1991   Alicia is proclaimed in Mexico prima ballerina assoluta of the Americas.

1995   On November 28, Alicia dances *Farfalia,* her last ballet performance.

1996–present   Alicia teaches, choreographs, and directs Ballet Nacional de Cuba.

2008   October 28–November 6, the sixtieth anniversary of the Ballet Nacional de Cuba is celebrated.

2010   On June 3, Alicia is honored by the American Ballet Theater in New York.

Arabesque: A ballet position with one arm extended in front and the opposite arm and leg extended behind

¡Ay, Dios mío: Oh, my God!

¡Baile!: Dance!

Barre: A long horizontal handrail that dancers use for support while practicing

Bravísimo: Very well done

Bravo: Well done

Cafecito: A small cup of coffee

Cenicienta: Cinderella

Chui: Whistling sound

Choreography: Art of creating, arranging, and recording the dance movements of a ballet

Clair de lune: By the light of the moon

Corps: Group of dancers

Danseur: Male ballet dancer

En pointe: Dancing on the tips of one's toes in special shoes

Escuela Nacional de Ballet: National School of Ballet

Fouetté: Quick whipping movement of the raised leg in ballet usually accompanying a pirouette

Guajiros: Cuban peasants

Habanos: Cuban cigars

Maître: Master teacher

Malecón: Sea wall

Mamá: Mother

Mariposa: A butterfly; a Cuban flower that resembles a butterfly

Museo de la Danza: Dance Museum

Pa'lante: Coloquial for "*para adelante,*" go on

Papá: Father

Pas de deux: A dance for two people

Pas de quatre: A dance for four people

Pirouette: A turning step performed on one leg

Prima ballerina assoluta: Unquestionably the best principal ballet dancer

Spotting: The technique of using eyes to focus on a spot to avoid dizziness as one turns

Zunzuncillo: Cuban bird

Sources

PUBLICATIONS AND INTERVIEWS

Alonso, Alicia, and Pedro Simón. *Diálogos con la danza.* Havana, Cuba: Editora Política, 2000.

Arnold, Sandra Martín. *Alicia Alonso: First Lady of the Ballet.* New York: Walker Publishing Company, Inc., 1993.

Bernier-Grand, Carmen T. Interview with Pedro Simón. Museo de la Danza, Havana, Cuba. October 28, 2008.

Bernier-Grand, Carmen T. Visit to Museo de la Danza, Havana, Cuba. October 28, 2008.

Bernier-Grand, Carmen T. Rehearsal of *Sleeping Beauty* and interviews with students from Ballet Nacional de Cuba and L19 Alejo Carpentier. Gran Teatro García Lorca, Havana, Cuba. October 29, 2008.

Bernier-Grand, Carmen T. Interview with Ahmed Piñero Fernández. Museo de la Danza, Havana, Cuba. October 30, 2008.

Bernier-Grand, Carmen T. Performance of *Giselle.* Gran Teatro García Lorca, Havana, Cuba. November 2, 2008.

Bernier-Grand, Carmen T. Interview with Fernando Alonso. Escuela de Ballet Nacional de Cuba, Havana, Cuba. November 4, 2008.

Bernier-Grand, Carmen T. Interview with Miguel Cabrera. Headquarters of Ballet Nacional de Cuba, Havana, Cuba. November 5, 2008.

Bernier-Grand, Carmen T. Sixtieth anniversary of the Ballet Nacional de Cuba, Gran Teatro García Lorca, Havana, Cuba. October 27-November 6, 2008.

Bliss, Peggy Ann. "Alicia Alonso!" San Juan, Puerto Rico: *The San Juan Star—Portfolio,* February 20, 1983.

Cabrera, Miguel. *Festival internacional de ballet (1960-2004): Una cita de arte y amistad.* La Habana, Cuba: Editorial Letras Cubanas, 2006.

De Gamez, Tana. *Alicia Alonso: At Home and Abroad.* New York: Citadel Press, 1971.

Horosko, Marian. "Alicia Alonso 'The Flower of Cuba': Diary of a trip to Havana." *Dance Magazine,* August 1971.

Levin, Jordan. "Revolutionary Moves." Los Angeles: *Los Angeles Times,* January 12, 1998

Mili, Gjon. "The Ballet." *Life* magazine, March 20, 1944.
Simón, Pedro. *Alicia Alonso: Órbita de una leyenda.* Madrid: Artes Gráficas, ENCO, S. L., 1996.
Siegel, Beatrice. *Alicia Alonso: The Story of a Ballerina.* New York: Frederick Warne & Co., Inc., 1979.

DVD

Alicia Alonso: Prima Ballerina Assoluta. Producer Allan Altman, executive producer Ernest Gilbert, Video Artists
    International, Inc. DVD, 2005.

Websites

" Alonso, Alberto." Telegraph.co.uk. (August 1, 2008)
        http://www.telegraph.co.uk/news/main.jhtml?xml=/news/2008/01/08/db0801.xml
Alonso, Laura. "Laura Alonso: Master Teacher Extraordinaire," www.lauraalonso.net
Boccadoro, Patricia. *CultureKiosque.* "National Ballet de Cuba." (October 26, 1998)
        http://www.culturekiosque.com/dance/Features/rhcuba.htm
Campoy, Ana. *Cubans 2001.* "Ballet: Cuba's Enduring Revolution."
        http://journalism.berkely.edu/projects/cubans2001/story-ballet.html
Estrada Betancourt, José Luis. *Juventud web rebelde.* *"Alicia Alonso jamás ha dejado de bailar."* (March 5, 2006)
        http://www.juventudrebelde.cu/2006/enero-marzo/mar-5/index-alicia-cultura.html
Lopez, Rodney, translator. *CubaNews.* "Alicia Alonso Visits the Canadian National Ballet." (December 27, 2007)
        http://archives.econ.utah.edu/archives/cubanews/2007w52/msg00114.htm
Marquez Herrera, Roxana, translator. *Cubarte.*
        http://www.cubarte-english.cult.cu/global/imprimir.php?currettable=entrevista&id=1923
Marshall, Margaret, and Anjuli Bai. *Ballet.magazine.* "Alicia Alonso Prima Ballerina, Ballet Nacional de Cuba." (March 6, 2008)
        http://www.ballet.co.uk/magazines/yr_03/nove03/interview_alicia_alonso.htm
Reloba, Dafné, and Claudia Delacroix. *Sol y Son* magazine. *"Fernando Alonso: la inteligencia en los pies."* (July 1, 2005)
        http://www.solysonmagazine.com/item.php?lang=2&issue=89&item=6&contentPage=2
Ross, Ciro Bianchi. Cubanow.Net. "Alicia Alonso: A Woman in Front of Her Mirror." (February 11, 2008)
        http://www.cubanow.net/global/loader.php?&secc=12&c=2&item=4209

Notes

Unga

Marianao: A town situated in a slightly hilly area on the northern coast of Cuba. Today Marianao is one of Havana's
    principal suburbs.

Mamá: Ernestina del Hoyo

Dresses: Ernestina del Hoyo designed and sewed many of Alicia's dance outfits, including her dress for the Spanish Dance in
    Swan Lake and Giselle's peasant dress: Bernier-Grand, visit to Museo de la Danza.
"Chui, chui,": Alonso and Simón, *Diálogos con la danza,* p. 90.
"Having Mamá": Estrada Betancourt, *Juventud web rebelde,* p. 7.

Papá: Doctor Antonio Martínez

"Papá is a good man": Alonso and Simón, *Diálogos con la danza,* p. 89.
"¿Cafecito, Doctor?": Ibid.
"Wear jackets": Siegel, *Alicia Alonso,* p. 5.
"Wear dresses": Ibid.

Flamenco

"¡Olé! . . . ¡Baile!": What a flamenco teacher would say.

Ballet Lessons

Ballet lessons: Yavorsky taught at Sociedad Pro-Arte Musical, managed by Laura Rayneri de Alonso, later Alicia's mother-in-law.
"Straight": Siegel, *Alicia Alonso,* p. 11.
"Backs flat": Ibid.
"No, head up, not back.": Ibid.

Cenicienta
"I'm standing on my toes": Siegel, *Alicia Alonso*, p. 14.

Grand Waltz
"Good.": Siegel, *Alicia Alonso*, p. 14.
¡Zas!: Alonso and Simón, *Diálogos con la danza*, p. 93.

First Solo
"Better than chocolate ice cream": Bliss, "Alicia Alonso!" p. 40.

Fernando Alonso
Fernando: He studied business in the United States.
"My God!": Siegel, *Alicia Alonso*, p. 19.
"I'd like to dance": Reloba and Delacroix, "Fernando Alonso," p. 1.

Flaming Souls
Malecón: Fernando Alonso claimed that he never went to the sea wall. This is puzzling because the Alonsos lived nearby. Fernando's stepdaughter, however, reminded him that he did: Bernier-Grand, interview with Fernando Alonso. Alicia liked going to the Malecón. It was and still is customary for Cuban boys to declare their love for their girlfriends by the Malecón. So, although no one knows for sure, Fernando might have declared his love for Alicia there.
"For the love of God, will you join me?": A phrase from *Clair de Lune.*

Leaving Behind a Blue Childhood
"To be a professional ballet dancer": Bernier-Grand, interview with Fernando Alonso.
"In New York I will": Ibid.
"People will talk": Siegel, *Alicia Alonso*, p. 23.
"As soon as I arrive": Fernando Alonso paid for Alicia's trip. Bernier-Grand, interview with Fernando Alonso.
"Male ballet dancer": Ibid.
"From a good family": Ibid.
Pa'lante: Estrada Betancourt, *Juventud web rebelde*, p. 6.

New York City
Becomes Alicia Alonso: In Latin America women didn't drop their maiden name, but in the United States they did. Alicia, reluctantly, changed her last name from Martínez to Alonso.
"What a beautiful baby girl!": Reloba and Delacroix, "Fernando Alonso," p. 2. At the time that Alicia gave birth, husbands were not allowed in the delivery room, and visitors saw the babies through a glass window.

Debut on an American Stage
Ballet lessons: Alicia took private lessons from Alexandra Fedorova, a veteran of Ballet Russe, and Enrico Zanfretta, former master of the ballet school in Italy.
"I want that girl": Arnold, *Alicia Alonso*, p. 17.

Ballet Caravan
Laurita: Her uncle Alberto took her to Cuba: Bernier-Grand, interview with Fernando Alonso.
"Did you see that arabesque?": Siegel, *Alicia Alonso*, p. 41. Ballet critic Ann Barzel said of Alicia's arabesque: "It was extraordinarily beautiful—high, yes, but the right slender leg always out, the foot arched, pointing to infinity, the back and head high, the arms in line—without any tension.": Alonso and Simón, *Alicia Alonso*, p. 22.

Swarming Darkness
Dancing in a full theater: Alicia became ill during a performance. A doctor in the audience went backstage and told her she was suffering from a detached retina. She performed the last evening of the Ballet Theater's spring season and then went to the hospital. Siegel. *Alicia Alonso*, p. 50.

"You Must Not Cry"

Alicia's surgeries: She could still see, like a camera without focus, through a small hole in her left eye. Bernier-Grand,
    interview with Miguel Cabrera.
"You must not cry": Siegel, *Alicia Alonso*, p. 68.
"How can I stop living?": Alonso and Simón, *Diálogos con la danza*, p. 101.

Dancing Fingers

"I see the theater curtain open": Marshall and Bai, "Alicia Alonso," p. 4.

Raging Storm

"¡Ay, Dios mío, my eyes!": Siegel, *Alicia Alonso*, p. 71.
"You just have cuts": Paraphrase, Ibid., p. 72.
"Can I dance?": Ibid.
"It's up to you": Ibid.
"I am ready to return.": Ibid.

To See and Dance

"God does not intend": Siegel, *Alicia Alonso*, p. 79.

No Way

"Yes, I'll dance.": Paraphrase, Siegel, *Alicia Alonso*, p. 76.

Dancing Feet

"For history!": Arnold, *Alicia Alonso*, p. 43. The ballet paraphernalia collector was George Schaffe.

Doctor Martínez

Life: The March 20, 1944 magazine showed one and a half pages of photos of Alicia, pp. 82-83.
"One of the prettiest figures in ballet": The caption under Gjon Mili's multiple-flash photograph of Alicia doing a *pas de
    bourrée. Life*, p. 82.

Undertow

I'll never be that good: Siegel, *Alicia Alonso*, p. 78.
"Go see Alicia Alonso's Ate": Ibid., p. 80.
Markova's: Her real name was Lilian Alicia Marks but she changed it to Alicia Markova because audiences preferred
    Russian dancers.
"America's finest Giselle!": Arnold, *Alicia Alonso*, p. 51.

Ballet Alicia Alonso

Ballet Alicia Alonso: At first its dancers included Igor Youskevitch and others who had been laid off from Ballet Theater.
"Don't worry": Siegel, *Alicia Alonso*, p. 111.
"How did you do that?": Paraphrase, Ibid.
"The hotel's curtains": Paraphrase, Ibid.
"Doesn't our government": Ibid., p. 112.

Ballet de Cuba

"I cannot live": Siegel, *Alicia Alonso*, p. 113.

Fidel Castro

Fidel: Castro was accompanied by Antonio Nuñez Jiménez, friend of Fernando and Alicia, fan of Ballet de Cuba, and
    topographer of Ché Guevara. At that time, Alicia was dancing with Ballet Russe in Chicago.
"It's so late": Horosko, "Alicia Alonso," p. 56.
"I forgot what I came for": Ibid.
"One hundred thousand dollars": Ibid., p. 57.
"I'll give you two hundred thousand": Ibid.
"Two hundred thousand dollars": Cuban exiles say that the money belonged to the people of Cuba and it wasn't Castro's
    to give.

Banned
"All my hopes and dreams": Bernier-Grand, interview with Miguel Cabrera.

Latin Temptress
Maya Plisetskaya: During a Ballet Nacional de Cuba tour in Moscow in 1966, Maya asked Alberto to choreograph a special *Carmen* for her, using the music of Maya's husband, Rodion Shchedrin. Alicia demanded that he choreograph a special *Carmen* for her, too.
"You must choreograph *Carmen*": Paraphrase, "Alberto Alonso," p. 1.
"Maya's *Carmen*": Ibid.

Prima Ballerina Assoluta
Denmark: This incident happened in 1969 while rehearsing with a Danish company in Copenhagen. Arnold, *Alicia Alonso*, p. 82.
"The most moving and sweetest Giselle": Bernier-Grand, interview with Miguel Cabrera.

Beloved Ballerina
WHY DO YOU: Nobody can remember exactly what the protesters' posters said because of being focused on Alicia's return to the United States. The sayings here have been taken from a blog by an angry Cuban exile.
"Artists have roots": Horosko, "Alicia Alonso," p. 54.
"Alicia!": Arnold, *Alicia Alonso*, p. 87.
WELCOME: The banner is a white cloth with black letters. Bernier-Grand, visit to Museo de la Danza.

Ballet School
"You must feel the rain": Multimedia: "Sapheads Staged by Laura Alonso."
"You must feel the wind": Ibid.
"Your students": Multimedia: "Laura Alonso—Male Class."
"You are brilliant, Mamá": Paraphrase, Levin, "Revolutionary Moves," p. 14.
"I'm still learning": Paraphrase, Horosko, "Alicia Alonso," p. 54.

Farfalia
"I will never announce my last performance": Bliss, "Alicia Alonso," p. 40.
"That was the last time": Marshall, "Alicia Alonso," p. 4.

"I Still Have Time"
"I Still Have Time": Ross, "Alicia Alonso," p. 1.
"How would you like": Ibid., p. 6.
"I'm telling you": Ibid.

Prima Ballerina Assoluta (Biography)
"I was all over the island": Boccadoro, *CultureKiosque*, p. 2.
"We had Alicia": Campoy, *Cubans 2001*, p. 4.
"Alicia wanted all the good roles": Ibid., p. 5.
"Alicia and I started:" Ibid.
Fernando: After his divorce from Alicia, he left to direct the ballet school in the Cuban province of Camagüey, but in 2000, he returned to Havana and is teaching at the Escuela Nacional de Ballet.
"Ah, my pointed slippers!": Marquez Herrera, *Cubarte*, p. 4.
"I imagine the ballets deep in my mind": Ibid., p. 2.
"Do you think Picasso died?": Bernier-Grand, interview with Miguel Cabrera.